T0128988

Feathers From Heaven

R. Alan Krum Jr.

TRAFFORD
PUBLISHING

Order this book online at www.trafford.com
or email orders@trafford.com

Most Trafford titles are also available at major online book retailers.

Printed in the United States of America.

ISBN: 978-1-4669-0149-0 (sc)

Trafford rev. 11/12/2011

 www.trafford.com

North America & international
toll-free: 1 888 232 4444 (USA & Canada)
fax: 812 355 4082

CONTENTS

In memory of: Carroll Lee Matthews and Dr. William Dean Wehunt
Two faithful servants of Jesus Christ whose shining example
still burns brightly in all of our hearts

My Prayer for You

My prayer for you is the strength to endure
For patience to react in kindness
Wisdom that God is in control of all things
Knowledge of Christ's presence
He is nearer than the air you breathe
Your work now is what He needs you for
He has not forgotten your dreams
He holds them in the palm of His hand
In His time all things will come to pass
My prayer for you is to realize that you are loved
His love never fades
It is infinite

Isaiah 40:31

The Solid Rock of Jehovah

The Lord is my strength and my shield
He protects me from harm
My soul rests in the arms of God
For He is my provider
In a world of darkness God is the one true light
He lights my path so I will not falter or faint
My hope is found in the solid rock of Jehovah
For He will not be moved
He satisfies the desires of my heart
For God is my salvation
I will trust and not be afraid
The Lord Jehovah is my strength and my song
His love never fails

Psalms 37:3-5
Isaiah 12:2, 26:3-4
1John 1:5

Hold His Hand

I don't know where to start or what to say

I just want you to find your way

I know you think life is not fair

That those you love are unaware of the depths of your pain

All I know is God knows you hurt

He has seen your tears

He loves you with all his heart

For Jesus has been down the very road you are walking

He's been mocked and beaten by those He came to save

He has felt the heart wrenching loss of a loved one

Jesus never gives up on the broken hearted

Hold His hand and never let go

He will heal you and protect you

He will carry you in his arms

He will clothe you in His love

His Bleeding Heart

On a hallowed hill long ago the heart of God
Bled for all mankind
A love that surpasses all understanding
With His arms outstretched Jesus Christ
Became the atoning sacrifice for all children of God
Forgiveness spilled out from every fiber of His being
The nails that pierced the King's hands
The crown that dripped with blood
The lashings that tore His skin
The long walk carrying the tree
The silence at the trial
The cry of mercy for the scoffers
Jesus chose this path with a bleeding heart
A heart that loves those who deny Him
Rejoices when the lost find Him
In Jesus Christ love is not spoken
It is displayed
In Jesus Christ love is not a careless whisper
He is the risen King and conqueror of Lucifer's stronghold
A bleeding heart of love eternally infinite
Of this no one can compare

The Anchor

I know that you feel like you are climbing a mountain
Everything is flying at you like heavy rain
There is an anchor of solid rock that will never wane
A ship with a captain that never rests
His sails will cradle your weary spirit
The rudder will bring your smile back
Prayers of those who love you will give you strength
So you know that you are never forgotten
The sun will shine again
Lean on the anchor of peace and promise
He will provide everything you need

Tender Heart

A soft heart
A caring ear
Tears for the weak and weary
Clinging to the cross at all costs
A bleeding heart for the hurting
Quick to correct mistakes
Imperfect creature
Saved by grace
Sustained in God's strength
Unconditional love
A child at heart
Focused on the cause
To be more like Jesus
For His heart is the softest of all

Psalm 68:6
Hosea 11:1-4

Tears of God

Rain falls from the heavens as a storm blows through
Minds race with memories of departed loved ones
They wish they could still be here with us
God has called them into His presence for all eternity
The rain is their way of saying I wish you were here with me
I miss you
I love you
I will see you soon

Strength

Strength is smiling even when it hurts
Strength is realizing that God controls our lives and we don't
It is realizing that without Christ we are nothing
Strength is being on your knees before God at all times
Loving someone through the good and bad times
By that love both are stronger together
Strength is forgiving like an overflowing river
Strength is loving God with every fiber of your being
Strength is not going it alone, but allowing others to help
Strength is never giving up on love

Pure Joy

Searching high and low for an end to the pain
A way to stop the rain and lift the clouds of doubt
Running with no direction or purpose
In the valleys of life, God meets us
His blessed reassurance that all is well is found in the trials of life
He stands with us and carries us through the journey
All we must do is trust Him and have faith
Pure joy
Found only with the Prince of Peace, Jesus Christ
Pure joy, everlasting peace, infinite hope for each one of us

James 1

Let Your Light Shine

Let your light shine for the entire world to see
May it shine from the highest hilltop
And still be seen in the lowest valley
As you seek God's will for your life
Let your talents and gifts be your guide
With prayer and thoughtfulness seek Godly understanding
You have the love and support of family and friends
In His time May He fulfill the desires of your heart
When the times are tough
That is when your light will shine the brightest
For those who seek God with all their heart will find Him
As you begin this leg of the journey of your life
Always remember to let your light shine in the darkness
Spreading God's love and fulfilling all your dreams

Matthew 5:14-16, 6:33

Iron Eagle

An eagle can soar high above the storm
An eagle nests' on mountain peaks away from danger
Razor sharp claws like daggers claim fish from the sea
Long majestic wings display the strength of this marvelous bird
The eagle soars until a safe haven is found
It protects its young from harm
An eagle's call is the call of freedom, hope and determination
Steadfast and true
Like the red, white and blue
God's anchor of hope and peace
An eagle never quits until the task is finished
Perfection and precision is the motto in which he stands
True to God and country and his fellow man
A symbol of purity and grace
Faith that in every storm there is an eye of peace
Eagles are God's soaring ambassadors
Evidence that He is the almighty creator of heaven and earth
An Iron Eagle stands strong in the storm
Bearing the wounds with pride
For in time the storm will pass and everything will be made new
Eagles drive change and look to heaven and find ways to soar
Above the pain and trust God in all things and worship Him alone
Isaiah 40:31

Hopeful Hearts

Two hearts give their lives to God
Leaning on Him for everything and learning as they go
He Bible and prayer are their weapons against the enemy
Along the journey God gives them the greatest gift of all
Love
This love will endure through good times and bad
This love will conquer any obstacle in its way
A love rooted in Christ cannot fail
A love rooted in Christ is a witness to God's love for us
A love rooted in Christ brings hope in life's journey
Hopeful hearts from this day forward into eternity

Grace & Peace

I know that life is hard and you feel there are many hurdles

God is with you each step of the way

I know you have known sadness and loss

God's arms wrap around you always

I know you feel you have made mistakes

God has plans for your life and to prosper you

You are beautiful inside and out

You have many undiscovered talents

May God's grace and peace guide you all the days of your life

May you never forget how much you are loved

Jeremiah 29:11

Enduring Love

Two hearts joined together begin the journey of life
With only love for God and each other
Believing that a bond that is eternally connected cannot be broken
Through the years they live, laugh and love with each passing day
Holding each other through good and bad
Thick and thin
Knowing that together their love will endure and carry them through
Love's long journey

Power of God

Night falls on the troubled heart
A weary traveler has ended his journey
When you are at your weakest point
He replenishes your strength
When all hope is gone
He focuses your eyes towards the heavens
He shines light into the darkness
Those who seek His wisdom He never forsakes
For He is the giver of life
All things can be accomplished by the power of God

Brokenness

Broken at the cross
Man at his best
Relying on the Lamb to hike the journey
The Son is my compass
The father, my vantage point
Many don't understand
In weakness you are strong
In tragedy you will soar with the eagles
Live a life of integrity
A life of courage
A life of determination
A life of service to others
Hope restores brokenness
Faith endures pain
Love conquers all

Dry Your Tears

I know you wish you could hear my voice again

That you could hold my hand and I could hold you in my arms

You are probably thinking back on the many things I taught you

The Bible and prayer are weapons against the enemy

Your first bike ride

All of those memories into a river of love

Dry your tears

I am free of pain

The rain and storms in my life have ceased

I am resting in God's arms now

Jesus said, "Lay down your cross and trade it for a crown"

In Nicole's smile you will see me

In Karin's laugh you will hear me

Kathy and I have many long afternoons on God's couch to catch up on

I must tell her how much she has missed

Mostly, my love, don't forget Daddy loves you

My love never leaves you

It is tucked deep inside you

It is the blanket that warms you in the frigid air of life

When the sun shines warm on your face I am smiling on you from above

I love you all

Dry your tears

Love one another as I have loved you, we will meet again

It may seem far away, but someday Jesus and I will meet you at the gates of heaven

Dry your tears and smile and laugh, that is how you can honor me

On Solid Ground

You have been through trials and tests
Seeking God's will and following through on His promises
Life has been tough but you never gave up
The challenges only made you stronger
You stayed the course and finished the race
Showing your love for God through serving others
A humble servant
The knowledge you have gained will serve you in the future
God has many blessings in store for you
You can look to the future with hope and confidence
That He will never leave you in sinking sand
You are standing on solid ground

2Timothy 4:7–8
Hebrews 12:1

A Promise Kept

A promise is a word given to another
Jesus promised to never leave us nor forsake us.
As we battle through life, we must remember to put on the full armor of God
Practice prayer
Study the Word
Love one another always
When the end is near do not fear for it is a new beginning
Tears will flow, but the heart rejoices
For in death, there is new life in heaven
Be glad, for there will come a day when you will meet again
Hold on to the memories and one another
Remember the love you shared
For with Jesus hope never dies
It lives for all eternity with the Kings of Kings
For He holds the promise of life everlasting
One that will never be broken

John 14

My Song of Adoration

Oh Lord most high, I humbly raise my voice in song and praise

I have seen the majestic mountains and the rolling seas

I am amazed by your creation

I bow my head in reverence to you

By the smell and sound of the sea I am at peace

You have stilled my restless heart

This is my song of adoration

By your grace I have found rest

By your grace all my dreams will come true

I will never stop singing your praises

For you guide my steps and dry my tears oh Lord

This is my song of adoration

I love you for loving a wrench like me

You are never alone

As you walk through the fire do not fear I am with you
I am the God of protection
As you march into the battles of life I am beside you
I am the God of strength
As you face your weaknesses I will sustain you
I am the God of hope
When the nights grow cold and lonely I will hold you
I am the God of love
If you think you can disappoint me you are wrong
I am the God of mercy
You cannot run from me, for I will find you my precious child
I am the God of forgiveness
As my Son bared the cross I was right there with Him
I took the lashings and felt the nails
I cried when all was placed upon Him
I raised Him to life just as I will raise you out of the darkness
You are never alone

Isaiah 41:13

A Feather from Heaven

A tender ear to listen
A gentle touch to soothe
A word of advice when everything tumbles in your world
No matter what happens in our lives
Our mother is always there
She's the shining example of sacrifice, the eternal flame of love
Her love is from God above, unconditional, beyond compare
Like a feather from heaven the lessons learned
Fly through the breeze of time never leaving us
Instead they shape and mold us aiding in God's plan
Where would we be without our mothers?
Lost in the breeze like a feather from heaven

You Are Not Forgotten

I know times are tough right now
You feel you cannot see the sun through the clouds
Your heart aches for a loved one's pain
A rainbow after the rain
God is right beside you holding your hand
Holding you close
Helping you stand
You are always on my mind
You cares are lifted to heaven
For He knows your every need
He sees each tear
He hears each cry
On heavenly wings you can fly
With Jesus as our doctor
Healing will come
Comfort ever lasting
Practice patience and remember
You are not forgotten
You are burned in my memory
Through the strength and peace of Christ
You and yours are wrapped in His love

1 Peter 6:6-11, 2 Thessalonians 3:3

White as Snow

Pure white flakes fall from heaven
Each flake builds on the green grass
Flakes of peace
God's soft touch
His comfort calms all our fears
His arms hold us close to His chest
His voice is distinct
An open heart is its ears
Snow displays God's majesty
Each flake is unique
An individual portrait of the Great Craftsman
He is still God
He still controls all
All of us need to hear the music of our hearts
The song that God placed there
Call on Him and He will rescue you
He will make you white as snow

Isaiah 1:18

Thirsty

We all search for something to cure a deep longing
An ache that will not end
Comfort does come in things
Comfort comes from God
Through Jesus Christ
We find One that satisfies
Living water
He is the bread of life
With Christ you will never thirst
He is always there
He is always beside you
Filling your cup
Quenching your thirst

John 7:37

The Signature

A signature displays ownership
A sign of something bought and paid
Blood sweat and tears
Paid the cost
His hands signed the release of debt for the lost
A signature transfers blame and assures responsibility
God paid for me and you with the blood of His Son
A signature is a mark and record of services rendered
Jesus made His mark on man's heart
A love divine, bought and paid for in His blood
Our Doctor in the floods of life
Life is tough
Without the signature of Jesus Christ
Life is meaningless
Life is without purpose

1 Corinthians 7:23

The Life Inside

We have been waiting for you
Loving and holding on
Cleaving together in all that life brings
Sprinkles of grace from above keeping us together
We have been praying for you
As our love for each other deepened
Jehovah, the Great Provider smiled upon us
This is my gift of love to you
You can be trusted with the small things of life
The life inside will show you how much I love you
With this gift may you realize the cost of the cross
Its outpouring of grace
Its ever abounding love
The life inside
The love of two special people

Psalm 139

The Fabric of America

The fabric of America was torn apart that September day
Innocent countrymen died at the hands of those who
Oppose freedom, hope, gentleness and kindness for all
Her fabric was torn, but love mended it
Her strength was exhausted
The kindness of her fellow man rejuvenated her
She came back stronger than ever before
The fabric of America is like an iron eagle
No one can penetrate
Her armor is invincible
No source of evil can oppose or defeat
For this is God's country
He will not be moved
For in His strength
America soars like an eagle high above the tragic storm
Countrymen died, but not in vain
Horror was witnessed, but miracles rose from the ashes
Like an iron eagle in formation
America became one and made her fallen comrades proud

Isaiah 40:31

The Cross

The cross is a symbol of hope and forgiveness
The long beam displays a long way to sin
The short beam where the Lamb of God hung
Love was displayed with arms stretched out
My sin and your sin upon His shoulders
Blood was shed
Sins forgiven forever
Hope restored and access to the Holy God granted
When God looks at us, He sees His son
Jesus Christ our high priest; who sympathizes with all our iniquities
Who loves us despite our fallen ways, but now who was tempted
Without sin is with us, who gave us His all
Who gave His very life that all may live in harmony with Him
Hold on to the cross
It punishes sin and brings a sinner joy, peace and happiness
In a world of darkness the cross is a beacon of light
To all who seek
To all in need of hope
To all who choose God's path
For it is always best

The Church Bells Ring

A child of God takes the final breath of their earthly existence
Their spirit is carried up to heaven
The body is just a shell that holds the heart of the child
The soul is covered by the blood of the spotless lamb
Our Lord and master says to Jehovah, the great provider
"This is my servant who is blameless by my blood
Shed for their sins"
God opens his arms and pulls child to his chest
"Welcome home my child
I kept the light on and your bed is waiting for your sweet head"
On the highest peak close to heaven
The church bells rings, crashing like thunder
Another child of God saved by the grace and mercy of Jesus
They are now walking those golden stairs to the gates of home

Son Rise

Rise up out of the darkness
Tune out all the madness
Lean on the risen King
Your life has been made a new
His strength is sufficient to sustain all that comes your way
He will never stray from your side
Your works will not save you only the blood of Christ
Jesus, light of the world
Jesus, the giver of grace
He took your place
On the cross He thought of you
Son rise for you have been forgiven
Your tears are dry
Your heart is new
Broken for Him
Raised in newness of life

Matthew 28: 1-29
Rev. Mark A. "Keep the Son in your eyes" Adams
Redland Baptist Church, Rockville, Maryland

Standing in Line

Waiting in line to partake of the feast He prepared

This we do in remembrance of Jesus Christ's sacrifice for all

As the cup touches my lips I remember it was my sin

That caused Him to spill out His life on a tree for me

As my teeth grind the bread

I remember it was His body

Broken so I may have new life

With tears of reverence and adoration I cry out to my Savior

May I lead others to the knowledge of your love for them

In their brokenness may they come to your throne

As a father leads his son

The Son leads others in the way He was raised

We all stand in line waiting for God

He answers each of us with passion, mercy and forgiveness

We must stand in line before He will answer

Stand Tall

Stand tall and know that God is with you
Even through the pain of your own doing
God will help you stand tall
Lean on His understanding and not your own
Put your hope and trust in His strength and guidance
Where you are is where He wants you to be
Hold tight to the truth He has placed in your heart
Storms come and He is our shelter of calm
Our anchor in the flood
He does not forsake those who love Him
He does not leave them lonely
He brings pieces of Him so we want more
He raises us up to look to heaven and see His light of love

Philippines 4:13

Smile

Smile and let the sun shine in
Smile when your day seems dreary and grim
Many talents you have been given
With those many have been blessed by your grace and presence
Many have seen God's love through you
A smile shows you care
It lightens another's burden
I wish for you a smile that never ends
The innocence of a child ever lasting
A smile to see the beauty within yourself
For God smiles at the mention of your name
Never forget your friends and loved ones smile for you
In thought and prayer at all times
Smile and remember you are loved and cared for always

Serve in His Name

Take care of the body of Christ
Serve others like you were serving the King of Kings
Listen and be a friend
Know what is to be held in confidence and what is not
Be a peacemaker and bring others together
Spread the love of Christ to all you meet
Even those sleeping on the street
Be willing to be bothered
For you must bare your brother's burdens
Pray always
For it is God's power that moves mountains
Serve in His name
For with Jesus Christ we all have a purpose
Without Jesus Christ all are lost
Without special servants
His love cannot be spread

Saved by Grace

What do you see in the word Grace?
Five letters seem oh so simple
It is by those five letters that God the Father
Sent His only begotten son Jesus Christ into the world
For those who did not deserve His pardon
You and me and everyone who will ever be
Blood was shed so that grace could follow
Grace shallows pride like Jonah in the belly of the whale
Grace breaks the chains of bondage
Grace heals the pain of regret
For it is by His grace we are saved
By His grace we are truly free

Ephesians 2, 8-9
Jonah 1:17
Luke 14:11-17

Rose of Love

My face is gone from your sight
My hands can no longer hold yours
From heaven's window I want to blow you a kiss
So you know how much I love you
I cannot begin to tell you how the many years we have shared
Roll into one
It seems like only yesterday I asked for your hand
You have given me many wonderful years
Three beautiful and strong children
We have laughed and cried together
You have given me strength when I was weak
Burn this candle in my memory
When the nights grow lonely
The light will remind you I am always here
My love never leaves you
Like a rose's scent
It lingers on
Smile for me

I love you always
You are my rose of love

Peace like a River

I need peace like a river raging over the dam
Life is driving me under gasping for air
It feels like no one cares
On my knees is where the pleasant peace is found
On my knees I can climb into my Father's lap
He lifts my burdens and dries my tears
In a calm voice He says
"Everything is going to be alright
I am in control
You are in my will
You I love
To you I bring a river of peace"

Isaiah 30:15
1 Kings 8:56

Our Great Hope

God came down from heaven clothed in a human shell
A helpless child who would save His people from their shortcomings
An infant totally dependent on His mother's care for survival
Yet He was God in the flesh
Our Great Hope
The Messiah God
Old Testament prophesy told of His coming
Many wanted a King who would relieve physical oppression
God saw man's oppressed heart as a bigger problem
Only a spotless lamb would satisfy God's wrath
He sent His son Jesus to walk the path
To tell of the Father's love for all
To Him we ask forgiveness when we fall
Last before God's son's journey was complete
He had to suffer on a tree
All was placed on Him
All to Him we owe
His reward is to tell others how He has changed our lives
Our great hope
The Lord and master of our hearts

Matthew 1:18–25

One True Light

Many years ago, the Creator had a plan
He spoke and light appeared
He molded the heavens and Earth
All that is living and gone is His
He laid the plans for humans to have a doing existence
All was in Adam and Eve's hands
Man was granted free will by God
The freedom to choose God's way or his
We all know he chose the wrong path
God had a solution for Adam's fall
He would come to Earth as a baby
He would grow, become a carpenter
Nails, hammers, blood and bandages
The Carpenter who builds would become the one who saves
He would let the hammer drive the nails into His body
All for love's sake
He would break the bondage of man
All authority given to Jesus Christ, the carpenter, the Son of God
His way is the only way to peace
One true light that leads the weary and lost home
It burns brighter than any star in the sky
Hope like a shining star
One true light

One

Since the beginning of time, God has had one solution for all things
Jesus Christ
We have a Father whose love is beyond definition
A Holy provider of a way back
To turn away from our sin
God sent His most prized possession
His son into the world
To redeem and reconcile the human race back to Him
Jesus went to the cross on His own free will
For He is God in control of all things and the one commanding creation
He calmed the seas when Peter cried out in fear
He healed the blind and demonstrated the matchless grace of God
He raised Lazarus from the grave
Death has no power over Him
He arose on the third day just like He said He would
No promise broken and no child of God left behind
One Faith, One Blood, One Savior
One Eternal hope

John 14:6

Never Ending

On a hill many years ago, God displayed His never ending love

His son, Jesus Christ was entrusted with all sin for all time

The nails through his tender flesh bled for all

He has the keys to death, for He arose

He healed the sick and made the lame walk

He cast the demons into a herd of wild pigs

Jesus, God among us

The one who still can change lives today

Whose Spirit guides those He loves

Light of the world into darkness came

God the Father, provider and sustainer

His love never ends

It is beyond compare

A love so hot, it burns those who resist it

A love so hot, it cools those who are healed by it

Love, never ending love

Romans 8:35-39

Matthew 8:25-34

My Wish

My wish for you is to find the true calling of your heart
For you to know God's will for your life
I wish for peace to resonate through the valves of your heart
A stillness to come over you as God carries you on your journey
I wish you never forget the love of friends and family
Happiness is their greatest wish for you
I wish the eyes of your heart see the beauty within yourself
Let your light shine from the highest mountain to the lowest valley
I wish that your mind and body is reminded of God's love for you
Even in the dark days of life there is light
All who seek the Light of the world will find it
Jesus is the greatest wish anyone could ask for
He is the wish that comes true every day without failure

My Love Abides

My love abides in those who follow me and my ways
It is there to comfort and console when the storms of life rage
When the tears fall
My love is the sunshine on your face
It holds the memories of loved ones lost
It remembers the good times
Provides hope for the future
Leans on the steadfast faith that all things work for good
Know that my love will hold you when you cannot stand
It will strengthen you when life is too much to bear
Abide in me and I will abide in you

John 15:10

Man of Faith

A man born by God's grace
A man who lived each day to its fullest
Hard times came and his faith in the Almighty grew stronger
A man who believed in the cause of Jesus Christ
A man who smiled when others would cry
A man who pressed on reaching for heaven
A man full of joy
A man full of abounding love
He is content with God's plan for him
His life reflects total dependence on God
His voice still lingers in the distance
"Come home to Jesus
He has everything you need"

Philippians 3:10-11, 21
Romans 8:35-39

Love without End

Love came down from heaven on a cold winter

Love of God displayed in the shell of a child

As the child grew, there was something different about the one called Jesus

He healed the blind and made the lame walk

He raised the dead back to life

His love never wavers

His heart bleeds for those who deny Him

He brings healing for the body and soul

A renewed strength that never fades

A remade mind that thinks of others before yourself

A new heart that will search for every single lost lamb

One who beckons all

Come home to me

I love you with all that I have

I stayed on the cross for you

I rose so that you may have new life abundantly

I will never leave you nor forsake you

My love has no end

I will come back for you someday to take you home with me

All you must do is call on Me first

Luke 15:10

John 9:1–41

Little Soldier

Standing tall in his young frame
A small image of his Daddy at attention
Love poured out through his tears
He salutes the silver eagle as it passes on its journey
A reflection of the First Son of 1963
He remembers the good times
Believes in a bright tomorrow
Shakes off the tears for a fallen hero
Places his portrait of honor inside the box
You do not have to serve in the armed forces to be a soldier
Life is a battle every single day
With God carrying us nothing is impossible
For He weeps when you weep and hurts when you hurt
Jesus stands beside you and holds you close to His chest
Stand tall little soldier
You are a lieutenant in the making
Listen to the words of your father
For his love is deep and everlasting
You have made us proud
Grandpa loves you very much

Luke 1:36-37
John 11:33-36

Joyful Noise

Joyful noise to lift the Lord our God on high
Drowning out the voices of hate, destruction and pain
Joyful noise to bring smiles and laughter to those in need
Joyful noise makes the memories of the past sweeter
Restoring hope, reaching in love and keeping the faith
Joyful noise resonating to the heavens
To praise our God, our Savior
The Giver of all of our joy

Psalm 98

Lean on Him

Fear and trembling haunt your every move
The enemy is upon you
Nowhere else to turn
Nowhere to run
Falling in deep despair
All hope seems gone
All seems lost
All is not
Lean on Him
The loving Son of God
The One who all hope resides
The One who we can always confide
Mistakes will be made
Some over and over
Keep fighting the good fight
Pressing on for a crown everlasting
He will sustain you through the storm
Lean on Him
Jesus
The lighthouse in the storm
God's rainbow after the rain

Psalm 55:22

Innocence

Innocence is found in the little things in life
Innocence is a child feeding his father a potato chip
Innocence is imitating your father's actions with every fiber of a little mind
Innocence is realizing when you have done wrong
Admitting fault with guidance
Innocence is being mesmerized by something new with such excitement
Innocence is having an open mind that is ready to be filled with knowledge
Innocence is realizing that there are two people that love me most
Mommy and Daddy
As we grow we lose that innocence
We neglect those we love
We are prideful
New ideas and sights do not excite us
We focus on ourselves and not on others
May we remember that Jesus said,
"The greatest commandment is to love one another."
He also said that we must come as a little child
In order to be first you must be willing to be last"

Matthew 18:4
Matthew 23:11

A Spirit to Serve

The calling of the heart to serve others and not be served
To sacrifice precious time so that each individual is completely satisfied
One who will not rest until their very best is displayed for all to see
Serving from the heart willingly
Correcting mistakes and learning from them
By those short comings character is strengthened
A spirit that never settles for second best
A spirit that breathes compassion and understanding
A spirit with a memory and no one is forgotten
A spirit that seeks to drive change and accepts what cannot be changed
A spirit that seeks to bring a smile to everyone they meet
Service is realizing that without someone to serve the heart has no purpose
It is a daily task to lay down your burdens and carry others'
By serving others with joy and compassion
You have fulfilled the great commission
Each day is another opportunity to exercise your spirit to serve

In the Garden

In the garden the Son of God knelt in prayer
He was deeply troubled
He asked God to take the burden of His heart away
In his next breath Jesus said, "Not my will, but yours."
Sweat and blood poured from His forehead
As the hour grew near
The cross was awaiting His ransom for the sins of all mankind
Without a word Jesus met His betrayer
He took up His cross for love's sake
He endured the pain and suffering for all of us
He turned to ashes the curse of sin and death
In the garden obedience to God's will was fulfilled
True love was displayed

Mark 14:32

From Your hands

From your hands I have learned many valuable lessons
You have helped me to climb many mountains
To tackle many challenges in my life
From your hands I have learned about sacrifice
To always do your best in every task you undertake
From your hands I have seen the love you have for all of us
From your hands I have never forgotten how much you love me
I hope by my hands you know how much I love you Dad

Jesus Still Matters

At the dawning of a new century, Jesus still matters

He came into the world on a cold winter's night to free the world from pain

To dry the tears of the lost and bring an eternal hope

More infinite than we will ever know

God knew His love was the only cure for sinful man

He loved us so much that He came in the form of innocence

A child, blameless with great joy

Emmanuel. God with us

Hope was here to stay

A savior who would suffer for things He had never done

A replacement for those who wronged and mocked Him

With Him you have everything

Without Him you have nothing

Forgiveness is not in what you do

It is in what He did

For it is by His blood that we exist

By His decision that we must die to live with Him forever

At the dawning of a new century the covenant is alive and well

The Savior's return is close at hand

Hope never dies in the eyes of Christ

For it burns with the purity of a blue flame

Penetrating the heart of sinful man

The reason for Christmas is Christ

The Alpha and the Omega

He still matters and He still reigns

I'm With Him

The voice of the Savior is calling out in the distance
If you listen you can hear His voice
The voice of the One slain by God for the sins of the world
He wants His people to come home
Jesus died so that all could live
He laid down His life in the name of love
He bore the pain and agony that man deserved
With His life He came to serve
For as we serve others we are serving Christ
His pain became our gain
He did all this just so we could say to God with tears of reverence
"I'm with Him"
For in Him we have everything
Apart from Him we are nothing

Ephesians 6:5-9
Philippians 4:13

I'll Miss you Friend

I'll miss you friend

I'll miss your strength, warmth and compassion

You were in my thoughts often for some reason

I only knew you for a brief season

Our encounter was small

Your impact on me is eternal

I remember your concern for those you love

The warmth you showed me as your guest

Our talks of submarines and sleds

Hope and faith

Strength and weakness

Most of all I remember your love for those you held dear

God, wife, daughters and grandchildren

I was in the presence of greatness

Greatness seldom found anymore

Strength beyond compare, strength known to come only from God above

Through His son, Jesus we are strong

Our roads are long you said

Keep the faith and be glad for your life

Love and you will be loved back

God is here through the laughter and the tears

Fear not for God is beside you

Thank you for those words

I'll miss you friend

Give God a hug for me and bow before the King for me

I'll see you soon and miss you always

Angel of Hope

All my life I have treasured the time we have spent together

You have given a love for God that sustains me all my days and nights

Through your walk with Him I know that He is in control and I am not

I have learned from you what it means to trust the Lord with all your heart

As the years go by, I cherish the beacon of peace that you have given to me

Your faith in me is unwavering even when I lose faith in myself

I hope there is never a day when you do not feel loved

The list is unending of the many blessings I have because of you

You have been an angel of hope in my life

I wish you many more peaceful days to come

I Hope you Smile

I hope you smile and remember you are loved
I delight in you just as God does
Hard times come, but God is in control
I hope you smile
God is bearing the burden with you
For He made you in His image
To glorify Himself
For your smile can bring joy to all you meet
I hope you smile
You are in my prayers and never forgotten

I Will Remember You

You have helped me through many trials
We celebrated many triumphs in my life
I will use the lessons I have learned to keep your memory alive
In my child's smile I will remember you
When they laugh I will remember you
I may have not told you enough that I love you
But my heart bleeds with love for you
I will hold you in my heart forever
Ride high into Heaven's gates
May you dwell in the house of the Lord forever
I love you, Dad . . . .

Hold His Hand

I do not know where to start or what to say
I just want you to find your way
I know you think life is not fair
That those you love are unaware of the depths of your pain
All I know is He knows you hurt
He has seen your tears
He loves you with all His heart
For Jesus has been down the very road you are walking
He has been mocked and beaten by those He came to save
He has felt the heart wrenching loss of a loved one
Jesus never gives up on the broken hearted
Hold His hand and never let go
He will heal you and protect you
He will carry you in His arms
He will clothe you in His love

A Man of Great Hope

A man of great hope
Focused on the promise of tomorrow
A man of contagious faith
Carrying his cross daily through trials and triumphs
He was loved by all who knew him
He gave love straight from his heart
Honesty and integrity flowed in his daily life
No matter what came his way
He always believed in the will of God
He always looked to the future
With great hope and promise

Texas Toast

He hailed from the tumbleweeds of Texas
Bringing hope to the lost and wandering
He held his Bible close to his heart
The love of Christ flowing through his veins
He heard the call in the distance
"Come to the Nation's Capital
There are souls to be saved"
He packed his boots and hat
Mounted his horse
Following the King's calling here in the city of Rockville
He guides many to the cross
He is there when there are hurts and joys
Even for the little girls and boys
A southern drawl to his words
He is a messenger of hope and peace
A faithful friend
A lover of Texas toast

An Angel by My Side

All my life I have known that you loved me

You have watched me grow from a young boy to a young man

You have helped mold me into the man I am today

I owe my life to you

For without your guiding hand beside me I would fall

Even today I still need your guidance and wisdom

As children grow

They never lose the need for a helping hand

Although they sometimes forget to ask

You have been the angel by my side

You have never left me even when I have pushed you away

On this special day

I want you to remember

My love for you will never end

I will stand beside you as long as God allows

The Tears will End

I know you think your life is over and all is lost
That your love is dried up and gone
I am here to tell you that the tears will end
Soon you will be out of the valley
Soon you will be soaring with the eagles
I have not left your side
I am carrying you through
In Me your strength is renewed
In Me your love is restored
Let go of the hate
Lift your head up to heaven
Jesus is here
The mighty King who dries all tears
The tears will end my child
Your smile will return

A Tender Ear

Since I was young you have been a tender ear in my life
A tender ear to listen to all my trials and troubles
You have seen me through many storms
Rejoicing with me when the sun shines again
Through your eyes I see the world with a loving heart
Know that as long as I try my best every day
God will do the rest
There is no measure I can use to repay you for all you have done
I just know that I am one of the lucky ones
Heeding your advice is my reward
It molds me into a better man everyday
As long as I have you in my life
I will cherish your tender ear

Love will find you

I know right now your heart is aching
You feel betrayed and lonely
You have lost your one and only
He failed to see the beauty deep inside you
The things that make you special and unique
He fell for a vixen of the night
He forgot the lady who waits for him
Love will find you
He will be everything to you
He will fulfill all your dreams
Do not fear
Do not cry for long
Love will find you
Love never fails

1 Corinthians 13:4

Children are God's Little Angels

God made children so adults could see them as His special servants
They see straight to our hearts
They laugh and play in joyful noise
Just being ordinary girls and boys
Children see things that adults cannot
A child is a picture of innocence and a willingness to let go
To let a strong and experienced hand guide them
That is the way Jesus Christ intended it to be
For it is written, "We must reach for Him just like a child"
We have been given a gift
Children are more precious and valuable than all the wealth in the world
God gives us wealth, but most of all He gives us love
We see His love through the eyes of a child
Through their reflection of God's unconditional love
We bare witness that children are God's little angles

Endurance

Pain and tears falling down like rain
Trying to make it
Trying to change
Pulling the heart strings
Holding on to the faith
He will keep you safe
He will be your shelter
He will let the sunshine in again
Lift the clouds away
Endurance builds character
It makes the weak strong
Molds the human shell into a man after God's own heart
Walking through the fire without fear
Carried by the hands of God
He is always near
Enduring the burden with you

Acts 13:22

His Silence

The love of God displayed in silence
Jesus was betrayed by a friend for silver and gold
His words were few as He was led like a lamb to slaughter
He took His mission seriously and remained silent
As the charges were read, He knew what the soldiers were thinking
He did not answer to man
He answered to His father's will
The commander of His destiny
As the whips tore His skin beyond repair His heart was ready
Each drop of blood was cleansing the stain of sin on the human race
As the nails were driven in His hands and feet
He bore the burden with courage and determination
He only cried "Abba," as the weight of His task grew so painful
It was not the pain of the wounds, but the separation from God
With a crucified heart, Jesus remained on the cross
He remained there until it was finished and bore our burdens alone
He gave his all for all of us
Silence is a gift
God is always watching
He is there in the silence

Brother Bear

You helped me along when I was young
You sheltered me from harm
My rock in times of trouble
A pillar of strength that never wavers
Although the storms of life caused you pain
You never complain
For you know all things work for good
For those who love God and are called according to His purpose
My love for you grows stronger everyday
If I could ease your pain, I would
I pray that you have peace
I pray for your healing
Most of all I pray that you never forget God's love for you
By His love you and I are bonded forever
I am who I am because of you
My brother bear

Romans 8:28–30

Don't Cry for Me

I know you are sad that I am not here and hope that I would reappear
I have gone to be with the keeper of my soul
Jesus said, "My work here is done
Now I can trade my cross for a crown"
I was lost, but now I am found
Forever all my love for you will make a joyous sound deep inside your heart
In a child's smile you will see me
In a whisper of the wind you will hear me
When the nights grow cold and lonely
My memory will hold you
Most of all I will never leave you
My spirit watches over you always
Don't cry for me for I am with Jesus
The one who loved me first
In Him my tears are dried
I will see you soon
Don't cry for me
Smile

Crucified Heart

A soft voice to calm fears
A faithful friend who always listens
Counsel to those who seek
Solid rock of eternal strength
Light of the world revealed in miracles
Great Physician who heals the body and soul
Infinite hope
Conqueror of Lucifer's stronghold
Sin destroyer
Crucified heart
Crucified life
Jesus Christ, the one sacrifice for all
He lives in the hearts of those who seek and follow him
His kingdom will remain while all others will fall
Amazing love that redeems the lost and restores the saints

Psalm 18:3

Fear Not

Just as the angel came to the shepherds and said

Fear not, I bring you tidings of great joy, a savior to save all from sin

God says to each of us

Fear me and not man

Hold on tight to my truth

Put your hope and trust in my ways

Lean not on your own understanding

Acknowledge me in all you do and I will light your path

Fear doubts

Faith believes

Fear cripples you

Faith stands tall and shines like a lighthouse on a distant shore

God is a light in the storms of darkness

God is the light of trust

God is the light of truth

His light is never absent in the face of our worst fears

Acts 18:1-22:29

Arms of Strength and Comfort

Arms of strength and comfort to hold you in this time of sadness
Arms to lift up to heaven and remember her with gladness
Arms that carry the burden of a love gone before your eyes
Arms that rise in praise of her life that she has lived by God's grace
A hand to dry the tears you cry because you miss her smile and touch
A hand to hold, as you walk the path without her
Hands to place the images around you to remember her
Hands to pray for a healed heart and mind
In Christ, we have a good shepherd who is always there
He is our strength and comfort
Because He lives you will see her again
She is healed and resting in the arms of God
May the loving arms of Jesus Christ comfort you
May He be your rock
May you rest in the hope that with sadness
There will soon be joy
With tears there will be laughter
With Jesus you can always face tomorrow

His Hands of Grace

It was planned into existence since the moment God made the world

His hands of grace would save his people and reconcile them back to him

For He is good and his mercy abounds for the unrepentant heart

He puts obstacles in the path of the lost so they find the light

Try to go it alone and human strength will fade

In His hands strength is infinite

His hands of grace beckon you home

His hands of grace that draw you to the cross

By His hands all who believe are redeemed

By His hands mercy is granted

His hands of grace healed the sick and bled for all

His hands of grace never turn away those who cry out to Him

His hands carry the tired and downtrodden

His hands lift the burdens of the heart and bring peace

His wonderful hands of grace

A Thankful Heart

In the past I thought like a child
I behaved like a child
Over time, I grew in my thoughts and reactions
I found a new life
A new perspective on what really matters
God drew me to His side and said,
"This is my son, Jesus
He died so that you may live and have new life
Life full of abundance and promise
He will stand beside you and bare life with you
He will never forsake you"
God changes lives through Jesus Christ
As His children we should come to Him always
With a thankful, repentant heart
Thanksgiving is not a day
It is every day of our earthly lives

Psalm 103
Hebrews 13:5

Look in My Heart

Look in my heart O' God and search every corner
Bring to light the scents that are not a sweet fragrance to you
Bleed my mind of imperfections
Control my tongue so that others may hear only words of hope
Harness my hands to lift up and not tear down
When darkness shows its face
Fix my eyes to heaven for your strength and guidance
I can only make it if you carry me

I am Beyond all of Your Pain

I am beyond all of your pain
I am the rock you can lean on
I am your great hope
I am infinite strength
I am the God of second chances
I am the God of forgiveness
I have conquered death
I have broken the chains of bondage
You are free as long as you abide in me
You are forgiven
You I love
I delight in you
I will carry you through it all
I am beyond all of your pain

Isaiah 26:3–4
John 14: 26–27

Give me an open Road

Give me an open road to clear my head of all distractions

Give me eyes to see all your attractions

Give me a throttle with lots of speed so I can run with you

Give me a memory of your love for me always

Give me peace and your understanding

Give me the arms of my wife wrapped around me

She shows me your love

Give me an open road of infinite distance

So I never forget Lord Jesus how much you love me

A Giver's Heart

Lord God you want my all
Nothing held back
My help when life becomes too much to handle
If giving to you does not cost me something
It does not satisfy you
You want a giver's heart
A heart that loves you with all its strength
A heart that bleeds for you alone
A heart that will show the love of Christ at any cost
Reaching out to the lost
For as long as I give I will receive so much more
A giver's heart can restore a lost soul
To bring God's child back into His arms

Psalm 24:1

His Great Faithfulness

No one is above Him for He is the Alpha and Omega
The beginning and the end
He never grows weary or weak
Longs to be a friend to the meek
His love is an ever flowing stream
His grace astounding
It leaves the heart pounding
Seekers of the truth He desires
Ones with their hearts on fire for the cross
Never counting the cost
You cannot run from Him
For He sees all at all times
Forgiveness with open arms
Keeping us safe from harm
Strength that never fades
Eternal flame of hope
A shady spot from the heat of life
Great is His faithfulness
For He is God and He is always good

2 Timothy 2:13
Job 4:18
Lamentations 3:23

Holy One

In the little town of Bethlehem a child was born

This was no ordinary child

This child was the only Son of God

He would one day become a carpenter

With blistered and bloodstained hands from the nails and wood He crafted

He would bring sight to the blind and calm the raging sea

He would heal the sick and raise the dead to newness of life

On a cross He would take away all the sins of the world

Past, present and future

He is the compass for all who need direction

Holy child born of a virgin

God in the flesh

Holy One

Hope for Tomorrow

Since the beginning of time, man has searched for a guide in life
The Christmas star led the shepherds and wide men to the Messiah long ago
Since that time, we have had the privilege and honor of God's guidance
Through Jesus Christ God wants His created to abide in Him
Jesus said, "I am the true vine and my Father is the vinedresser
He prunes in me what does not bear fruit
The branches cannot exist without the vine
Abide in me and I will abide in you
Draw near to me and I will draw near to you
As we sail through life, we journey through trials and tribulations
Our golden yacht can become battered and tossed about in the high seas
God is our calmness through Christ who calmed the seas
He can also calm the seas in our lives
God wants to be our captain
We must be willing to be part of His crew
Trust His leadership through Jesus Christ at any cost
In this we will be a witness to the lost
He is faithful in all things and a lover of the weak and oppressed
Redeemer of the humbled
King eternal
Our hope for tomorrow

Matthew 8:23-27, John 16 23b-30, Colossians 1:11-20

You Hold the Keys

I have searched near and far for someone to stand beside me
Someone to listen and hear the cries of my soul
Now you are here and I thirst no more
God has sent an angel to walk with me
A beauty to ride in the saddle with this Tennessee stallion
I will promise to always be your man
To be the one you can lean on
Your wishes will come true one by one
I will love you with patience and kindness and a slow hand
Hold my hand precious one
I will not let you fall
You hold the keys to my heart

Be Still

It is hard to quiet the noise of the world to hear God's voice

We are pressed further down as the chatter of the world distracts us

In our weakness we fail to realize

To release control over to God

He is the potter and we are the clay

He uses things for good

To mold us into the likeness of His son

Although sometimes we cannot see through the hard times and tears

We will when the rain stops and the sun shines again

For I know the plans I have for you declares the Lord

Plans to give you hope and not to harm you

God is good all the time

When the worst happens

He turns the page in the book of your life

Acts 17:11

Hearts in Armor

Two hearts searching for an end to the lonely
Looking high and low for their one and only
The one who will satisfy the hunger deep inside
A partner who will stand beside not behind
One whose love will grow stronger with age
Together the world is their stage
Hoping in tomorrow
Believing in each other
Finding a ray of light in the darkness
She is his and He is hers
Love that no one can penetrate
A fortress of strength and truth
What God has willed let no one destroy
Hearts in Armor
Hearts in love forever until their last beat

Anchor of Peace

I saw your tears and wished for a hug
I saw you smile for past memories
I felt your strength as you wished him love
I learned of your faith in God's provision
Your faith told me God's will is always best
I wished for an anchor of peace
To hold your ship when the winds of life fiercely blow
To know that others will carry your burden
To give you time alone
Time with family
Time with the Father and Son
The anchor of peace never moves
It is rock solid like the strength of Jehovah
He is our provider and comforter
The Great Physician, Jesus Christ
An anchor of peace
So you remember I love you more
As you love me and except my ways
As I try to be Christ to you
May you never forget
Love is the anchor
God's platinum
The strongest there is

Heavenly Rose

I wish you a heavenly rose to brighten your day
A ray of hope to light your way
When times are tough a prayer of peace to lighten the load
Always remember God is with you every step of the way
Jesus goes before you and knows your every need
He will never leave you nor forsake you
For you are His heavenly rose

Hugs

You are not alone at this time

You are held in the Father's arms

His care surrounds you in a fortress of comfort

As you walk through the valley

He is right beside you

His tears are yours

He hears your cry

Your strength will never waiver in God's arms

He will supply your needs

He made you and knows all about you

God made hugs so you never forget the depths of His love for you

The harder you squeeze the stronger the love

The arms that hugged the cross to redeem us all

Are open to all who receive them

These arms console and warm us as we shiver in the frost of life

Psalm 29, 34

Matthew 6:25–34

God Makes All Things New

God has the power to restore

The power to rebuild lives

He polishes us to a shine

His power is from everlasting to everlasting

When the flood of life is too much to bear

He is our life vessel

When you feel you cannot go on

God is our reason for living

Wonderful counselor

Mighty God

Worthy to be praised

He raised His son Jesus Christ on the third day

He brought man unto Himself

He finds coal and turns it to diamonds

In Him we have the power to change

The power to love instead of hate

Our lives are changed by the love of God

For in Christ, all are a new creation

The old is made new and access to God's wisdom and power is granted

2 Corinthians 5:17